Professor Bumblebrain's Bonkers Book on...

GOD

Published 2010 by CWR, Waverley Abbey House, Waverley Lane, Farnham, Surrey GU9 8EP, UK.
Registered Charity No. 294387. Registered Limited Company No. 1990308.

See back of book for list of National Distributors.

Unless otherwise indicated, all Scripture references are from the Contemporary English Version (CEV).
Copyright © 1991, 1992, 1995 by the American Bible Society.

Editing, design and production by CWR

Printed in China by 1010 Printing International

ISBN: 978-1-85345-579-7

Professor Bumblebrain's Bonkers Book on... GOD

ANDY ROBB

CWR

Welcome, young reader! Allow me to introduce myself. I am Professor Bumblebrain, and you are most privileged to be receiving the benefit of my superior wisdom, intellect and er … what was the other thing? Oh yes, that's it … my brilliant memory. It goes without saying, but I will say it anyway, that I will require your complete and undivided attention throughout the course of this entire book. If you don't think you're up to it, may I suggest you put the book down right now and go and find yourself something a little less taxing to do.

If that sounds like it's you, here are a couple of my helpful and constructive suggestions.

Perhaps you could have a go at doing the world's easy peasiest crossword?

Go on, give it a try.

Across

1. The first letter of the alphabet.

Down

1. What comes before the letter 'B' in the alphabet?

I think those rules are all self-explanatory, so I will now move on to the subject in hand which, if you have been observant, you will know is *God*.

There are a few very important things that you will need to know about God before we go too far.

Firstly, you aren't Him. God, that is. If you've somehow got it into your head that you *are* God, can I please encourage you to dismiss the thought this instant.

God is God.
You're you.
End of story.

I'm sure you're a very nice *you*, but that's simply not the point.

PLEASE DON'T TAKE IT PERSONALLY!

Dear old grannies knit patterned jumpers and buy you socks for Christmas, but when it comes to being God, they're simply not up to it.

Next up, you need to be made aware that God is invisible and you won't be able  to see Him however hard you try, so don't bother.

Yes, I know that this is frustratingly inconvenient, but please don't have a go at *me* about it.

That said, just because you can't actually see somebody, it doesn't mean they're not for real.

For example, I'll bet you've never ever seen the person who made your underpants, but do you lose sleep over it, wondering whether they really exist?
Of course you don't.
Well, I hope you don't!

My point is this: don't get stressed simply because you can't see the person who made the universe. (That's God, if you hadn't guessed already. And, no, just in case you were thinking of asking me, He didn't make your underpants. Well, not that I'm aware.)

God is there whether you know it or not. Between you and me, the Bible (a book about God) gives us a jolly big clue to help us see that God is there (even though we can't actually see Him).

THE BIBLE: A BOOK ABOUT GOD

Here's what it says ...

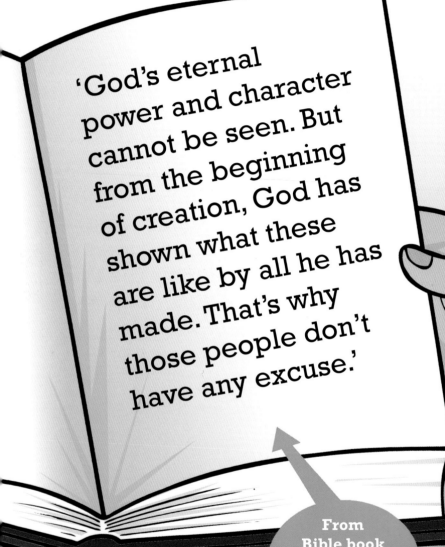

'God's eternal power and character cannot be seen. But from the beginning of creation, God has shown what these are like by all he has made. That's why those people don't have any excuse.'

From Bible book Romans, chapter 1 and verse 20

You'd think I was daft (you probably do anyway, don't you?) if I said that things like TVs , cars , computers , mobile phones , houses , clothes (and anything else you can think of) weren't made by someone, wouldn't you?
I think we'd *all* agree that this was a completely ridiculous notion.

We can look at something like a computer, and it will give us a good idea of what the people who designed it and made it were like.

I guess we'd say that they were clever, creative, imaginative and inventive, wouldn't we?

In the same way, when you look at a fish or a flower, a sunset or a sea lion, you can get a very good idea of what the person who made them is like. (That's God, just in case you weren't quite sure.)

So, that's what the Bible has to say about finding out what God is like.

Some people think the Bible is a work of fiction (that means a made-up story), but I can assure you that this could not be further from the truth.

When you have finished splitting your sides with laughter I will move on.

What do you mean, you didn't find my joke funny?
How very rude of you!
Don't you know quality when you hear it?

I'll have you know, I won the **'Funniest Brainbox of the Year Award 1982'** with this witty and clever joke ...

You don't get it? Oh, never mind. My superior wit is obviously wasted on you. I suggest you ask a science teacher to explain. Time to move on.

Another thing I need to tell you is that there is only one God but, and it's a very big but …

… **THERE'S ACTUALLY THREE OF HIM.**

Yes, you heard me right.
One God.
But three People.
You're completely confused, aren't you?
I knew I shouldn't have told you this
piece of information right at the start of
the book.

I WAS FORGETTING
THAT NOT EVERYONE HAS
A BRAIN THE SIZE
OF A LARGE CABBAGE,
AS I DO.

If it helps you to get your head around the concept, the three People I'm talking about are God the Father (whom this book is all about, if you hadn't guessed), Jesus (God the Father's one and only Son) and last but by no means least, the Holy Spirit. But the bottom line is that they're all God, they work together as one super-duper, tiptop, perfectly synchronised mega team, and because of that we refer to them in the singular, as *one* God.

That wasn't so difficult to understand, was it?

USEFUL INFO

The terms used for God being three People are 'the Trinity' and sometimes 'the Godhead'.

Now *that's* something to impress a grown-up with … except if that grown-up is me. It takes a lot to impress a man with a brain the size of a large cabbage, so I suggest you don't even bother.

If you can't get your head around the notion of God being *three-in-one*, you're just going to have to take my word for it and leave it there.

THE LAST THING I NEED IS YOUR BRAIN GETTING OVERLOADED AND EXPLODING ALL OVER THIS BOOK, SPOILING IT FOR ANYONE ELSE WHO WANTS TO READ IT AT A LATER DATE.

Oops, too late.
Oh well, never mind.
Right, moving swiftly on before
I get myself into any more trouble.
I have a question for you …

What comes into your mind when I say the word …

GOD?

Come on, quickly, we haven't got all day.
Your first thoughts please.
OK, now tell me, did you see an image of an old man with a long white beard sitting on a wispy cloud?

Or perhaps you thought of a horrible meanie who zaps people with bolts of lightning.

Well, if either of those thoughts popped into your head, I need to tell you that you're completely wrong.
Sorry to disappoint you but, as I will shortly demonstrate, God is nothing remotely like that. Before I enlighten you, though, please permit me to pass on to you a handy piece of information, namely …
God's address.

Yes, young reader, God has an address.
Before you ask, it isn't 52 Acacia Avenue,
Rose Cottage or anything twee like that.
God's address is … yes, you've got it …

No house number, no street name, just
'Heaven', plain and simple.

Heaven can't be found on a road map using Sat Nav or, for that matter, in a world atlas. You could travel from Tahiti to Timbuktu or from Wagawaga to Washington and never clap eyes on the place, because not only is heaven invisible to us mere mortals who live on planet Earth, but it's also located right outside of the whole whopping great big universe that we all live in.

Mind-blowing, is it not?

AND MAY I ALSO ADD THAT WHERE GOD LIVES, HE DOESN'T HAVE A MAILBOX, SHOULD YOU EVER HAVE THE INCLINATION TO SEND HIM A BIRTHDAY CARD OR SOME SUCH COMMUNICATION.

To be honest, it would be a completely pointless exercise anyway, because God doesn't have a birthday (because He was never born in the first place) …

… but we'll come on to that a bit later.

Now, here's the thing.

Dropping by to pay a visit to God in heaven isn't completely out of the question. Far from it!

God is more than happy for the likes of you and me to pop in to say 'Hi'.

It's always open house at God's place …

… at least it is for anyone who's got an invite. But there's just one small but rather important condition you need to understand before you pack your bags to spend a couple of weeks on vacation with God …

You've got to have died first.

Yes, I know that does make things a little bit awkward, but I'm not the one making the rules – God is. All this means that there's every chance that once you make it to heaven, you're probably not going to be needing a return ticket. Not unless, that is, you're like a guy from the Bible called Lazarus, who was brought back to life again (by Jesus). If you're not like him then, for sure, travelling to heaven is most definitely not going to be a round trip.

The good news is, that everyone gets a shot at ending up in heaven (with God) when they one day pop their clogs (die), but until then, we're going to have to make do with exploring what heaven is like from what the Bible has to tell us.

One thing that the Bible *does* tell us about heaven is that it's a jolly nice place to live.

FOR STARTERS, THERE AREN'T SUCH THINGS AS WARS AND FIGHTING, SICKNESS AND DISEASE, FAMINE AND HUNGER, SADNESS AND LOSS, FEAR AND ANXIETY, EARTHQUAKES AND DISASTERS OR, FOR THAT MATTER, ANY BAD STUFF.

In fact, when it comes to heaven, it's all good.

Welcome to Heaven

NO Brussels sprouts

NO homework

NO granny knitwear

NO horrid medicine

Once you've done that, you're probably halfway to imagining how awesome heaven is. Another thing you ought to know about heaven is that it isn't all angels sitting on clouds playing harps.

There's a lot more to heaven than that. In fact, to tell you the truth, it's *nothing* like that at all!

Did You Know …?

Heaven was around long before our universe was made, and it's just as real as the world we all live in. It's also got loads of things that we'd be familiar with, such as trees, the sea, fruit, rivers, cities, mansions and animals. In fact, almost a home from home. My guess is that everything we've got on planet Earth is just a brilliant replica of something that was already in heaven.

EVERYTHING?

Heaven is also the place where God sits on His throne and it's where He is worshipped non-stop. His awesome presence gives heaven all the light it ever needs, and fills the place with His love and power.

Talking of angels (which I was a moment ago, if you happened to have been paying attention), as well as people who've died ending up in heaven, the place is also full of all sorts of awesome and unusual heavenly beings, such as angels (man-like messengers of God), cherubim (weird winged creatures with animal-like heads) and seraphs (creatures with six wings). And forget it if you think heaven resembles some old church that's so quiet you could hear a pin drop.

You don't need to tippytoe around heaven for fear of upsetting anyone. Heaven's a noisy place!
At least it is sometimes.
If it wasn't enough that everyone in heaven seems to spend the best part of their time worshipping God at the top of their voices, there's also trumpet blasts and peals of thunder to contend with.
If your lugholes are a bit delicate, my advice to you is to collect a set of ear plugs at the Pearly Gates on your way in.

Did You Know ...?

God hasn't just got one name, as most people have (OK, I'm talking about first names here, so don't try and be clever) ...

What we're talking about here is bucketloads of names that each tell us something about *who* God is, *what* He does and *what* He's like.

For instance, one of them is **YHWH**. Yes, I know that because it hasn't got any vowels it's not exactly the world's easiest word to pronounce, but, on the plus side, it'll give you a high score in a game of Scrabble. Because YHWH was so difficult to say, people decided to make it into YAHWEH (pronounced YARWAY) which is much easier on the tongue.

YARWAY. YEP, MUCH BETTER, THANKS.

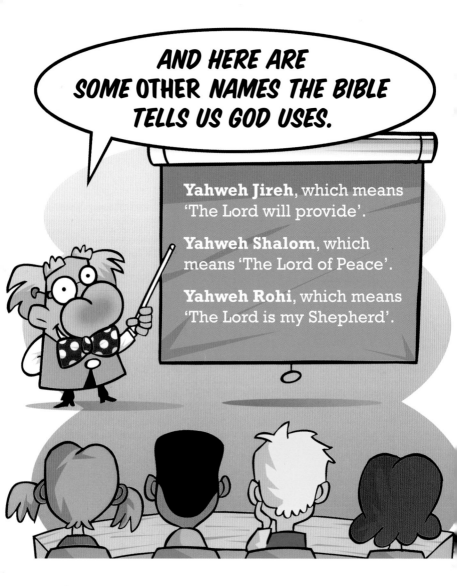

In fact, some smarty pants (though obviously not nearly as smart as me – that goes without saying) has worked out that there could be as many as 1,000 *different* names for God in the Bible.

Because God is so awesome and powerful, even just a sneaky peak at Him would probably kill you stone dead, so take my advice and don't try it! For this reason, God usually sends angels to deliver His messages instead. However, if He *does* show up, all you get to see is His glory (which is sort of like the dazzling light that surrounds Him).

For the purposes of this book, we will now take a look at a person in the Bible who had an unusual encounter with God, and see what else we can learn about Him.

THIS IS MOSES! I'M SURE YOU'VE HEARD OF HIM.

Amongst other things, Moses is famous for being the youngest person to sail up the River Nile single-handedly.

That's just a little joke of mine – chortle!

To cut a long story short, Moses was living in the desert, looking after his father-in-law's flocks when he noticed something rather strange.

A bush appeared to be on fire but – and here was thing – it didn't seem to be burning up.

Hmm?!

A burning bush was one thing, but what
Moses most definitely *wasn't* expecting was
for the bush to talk.
A river, perhaps, because it has a mouth.

A shoe, maybe,
because it has a
tongue.

A cup, even,
because it has a lip.
But a bush?
No way!

God was speaking to Moses from the bush …

The fire and the voice were God Himself, and Moses was commanded (by God) to take off his sandals because he was standing on holy ground.
Moses was terrified.
As Moses covered his face to shield himself from the glow of God's awesome power, God gave him a mission to free the Hebrew nation from slavery in Egypt.

THANK GOODNESS THAT'S SOMETHING I'M NOT GUILTY OF!

We will now fast forward a few years, to a time when the Hebrews had been freed from slavery and were wandering through the desert on their way to a new homeland.

God had decided that He wanted the Hebrews to meet up with Him, so they could get to know Him a bit better. What a splendid idea!

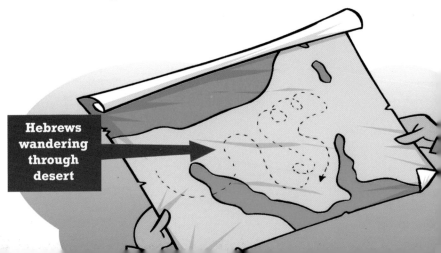

Hebrews wandering through desert

The place God had picked for the rendezvous was Mount Sinai.

There was nothing for it, it was going to have to be an *outdoor* meeting, because with two million Hebrews (give or take), there weren't any venues in the desert big enough to squeeze them all in. After two days of preparation, God finally showed up ... and big time!

For starters, just to whet the Hebrews' appetite, a big, black thunder cloud descended on the mountain (with a knee-knocking display of lightning thrown in for free).

Next up, just in case the Hebrews hadn't noticed that God had arrived, a loud trumpet blast (from heaven) just about knocked them off their feet.

But worse was still to come.
Just when the Hebrews thought that they'd been scared silly enough for one day, God decided to speak to them.
The Bible tells us that God's voice was like thunder.
They were just about wetting themselves with fright.
They couldn't take it any longer.
There was no way any of them were
in a fit state to meet up with God now.

MOSES COULD SAY 'HI!' TO GOD FOR THEM.

THEY WERE MORE THAN HAPPY TO STAY PUT AT THE FOOT OF THE MOUNTAIN, THANK YOU VERY MUCH.

So, Moses went it alone, and when he did finally come back down from the mountain (after a forty-day chinwag with God), his face was shining like he'd been out in the sun far too long but without any sun lotion on. Moses was radiant and shiny.

The Hebrews had gone and missed out
on a wonderful time with God.
Sadly, they hadn't cottoned on to the
fact that God wasn't out to scare them.
Far from it.
He just wanted to make sure they
understood how holy He was.
That was all.

Check out these fact files on some of the things God did (and which you can read about in the Bible) to see just how much power God's got.

What happened?

God created the entire universe including stars, planets, people, plants and animals.

How did it happen?

God simply commanded it all to come into being … and it did!

When did it happen?

Thousands of years ago.

Why did it happen?

Because God wanted to create something He could be friends with (that means people, just in case you weren't sure) and also a place for them to live.

God's Power
FACT FILE NO.2

What happened?
God split the Red Sea (between Egypt and Arabia) in two.

How did it happen?
God sent a powerful wind to create a pathway right through the middle of the sea.

When did it happen?
1500 BC (give or take a few years).

Why did it happen?
So that the Hebrew nation could escape from the clutches of the Egyptian army (who were chasing them) and get to the new land God had given them to live in.

God's Power
FACT FILE NO.3

What happened?
One of God's prophets called Elijah, challenged a bunch of guys (who worshipped the god Baal) to call on their so-called god to send down fire to burn up an animal sacrifice. Just for your info, Baal didn't come up with the goods, but Elijah's God did.

How did it happen?
God sent down fire from heaven and burnt Elijah's animal sacrifice to a cinder.

When did it happen?
Probably around 875 BC

Why did it happen?
Elijah wanted to prove, once and for all, that there was only one God. It sure worked!

What happened?

Jesus (God's one and only Son) had been crucified and laid to rest in a tomb. After being dead for three days, God brought Jesus back to life.

How did it happen?

God used His awesome power to give Jesus a new sort of body which could do things that normal human beings couldn't, such as walk through walls or suddenly appear from nowhere.

When did it happen?

About AD 33.

Why did it happen?

Because God wanted to demonstrate that Jesus had successfully completed His mission to patch things up between God and humans.

Right, young reader, it's time to get your brain around something a bit tricky. Are you up for it? Good! I've already rather helpfully told you where God lives, but allow me to bamboozle you with the mind-boggling fact that where God lives isn't actually *in time*, as you and I know it.

What I mean by that is, God lives in something called 'eternity'.

'Eternity' means going on for ever and ever and ever and ever and ever and ever and ever and ever and ever and ...

But it also describes something that has always *been there*, for ever and ever and ever and ever and ever and ever and ever and ever and ever and ...

Did you get that?

That's where God lives.

The line I have drawn represents time.
It's got a beginning and an end, just like
time has.

Before God made the world we live in (and the universe around it) there wasn't such a thing as time.
But as soon as God created the universe, time instantly began.

ARE YOU STILL WITH ME? GOOD!

The Bible says that one day time will end, which is why my straight line not only has a beginning but also has an end.
So, from my diagram on the previous page, we can see that God lives *outside* of time (in eternity) and we live *in* time.

Useful Info ...

Because God lives outside of time, He can see absolutely everything that's going to happen before it actually does happen, which is why you can read about God's prophets in the Bible predicting things that were going to happen long before they did (because God had already seen what was going to happen and had passed the info on to them). Clever, eh?

Prophet sharing some useful info

Now it might sound quite bizarre, but although God can't be seen by the naked eye and He doesn't even live in this universe …

Anyone can talk to God if they want to.

Yep, I'm not kidding.

Is that weird or what!

But before you whip out your mobile phone and send God a text, you need to know that you can't talk to Him as you would to your best mate.

And even if you could, the phone bill to heaven would probably be ginormous.

The Bible calls talking to God 'prayer', which is a word I'm sure you're familiar with. If you ever pray, you might feel as though you're talking to thin air, but rest assured, God can hear you loud and clear.

WHAT SORTS OF THINGS CAN YOU TALK TO GOD ABOUT?

Anything you like. You could tell Him what a brill God He is. You could ask for His advice in making an important decision. You could talk about school or you could ask Him to make someone who's not well better.

If and when you do take time out to get in touch with God, here's a heads up on some dos and some don'ts.

DON'T ...

Make it a one-sided conversation and do all the talking. Give God some space so He can talk back to you.

If you're a Christian, you'll soon discover that you can hear God's voice speaking quietly to your heart, and the more time you spend with God, the more you'll become familiar with what God sounds like.

DO ...

Expect God to hear your prayers and to answer them. The Bible calls that 'faith'.

DON'T ...
SPEND ALL YOUR PRAYER TIME GRUMBLING AND MOANING TO GOD.

Start by thanking Him for what He's given you, and ask Him to help you with your problems.

DO ...

Make sure that if you're asking God for something it's something you know He wants to give you. A good way of checking this out is by reading the Bible. It'll help you work out what's really important to God and what isn't.

DON'T ...

Babble on to God and try to impress Him by using loads of words. Keep it simple and from your heart!

Now, if you're scratching your head and trying to work out how on earth God can hear your prayers (let alone answer them) if He's zillions of miles away in heaven, let me help you.

But before I do, I'm going to need to teach you three new words.
Are you ready and alert?
Here we go.

The first word is …

It means … *all-powerful*.
It's a word which perfectly describes
what God is like.

This means … *all-knowing*.
It's another word which also describes what God is like – He knows absolutely everything. Yes, before you ask, that means even more than me.

Easy, young reader.

Because He's God.

God's not like us (as I pointed out to you at the beginning of this book, which you'd remember if you'd been paying attention). So, it's no big deal for God to be everywhere all at once. That's why He can be in heaven at one and the same time as He's doing stuff on Planet Earth. So that's how He can always hear our prayers. Because God is everywhere, because He's all-powerful and because He knows absolutely every last thing there is to know about anything, listen up to what I've got to tell you next.

It might come as a bit of a surprise to you, but even if you don't know God very well (or not at all), He knows you, through and through.
In fact, the Bible says that not only was it God who put you together in your mum's tum …

(OK, WOMB IF YOU WANT TO BE TECHNICAL)

… but also He knows how many hairs there are on your head …

God also knows every word you're ever going to say before you've even said them. When push comes to shove, there's no escaping from God.

If you think that sounds a bit scary, fret not! The only reason God is so interested in every little detail of your life is because He wants to get close to you so that you can get to know Him too.

Not only does He know you, but also He wants you to know Him as your heavenly Father and your Lord and God.

Being friends with God isn't quite the same as being best buddies with your friends at school.

Yes, God wants you to love Him, to talk to Him and to trust Him, but God also expects you to treat Him properly.

That doesn't mean you've got be scared of Him whenever He shows up or be worried about what He might do to you. No way.

To fear God simply means to respect Him and to obey Him.

After all, He is God, so I reckon He deserves it, don't you?

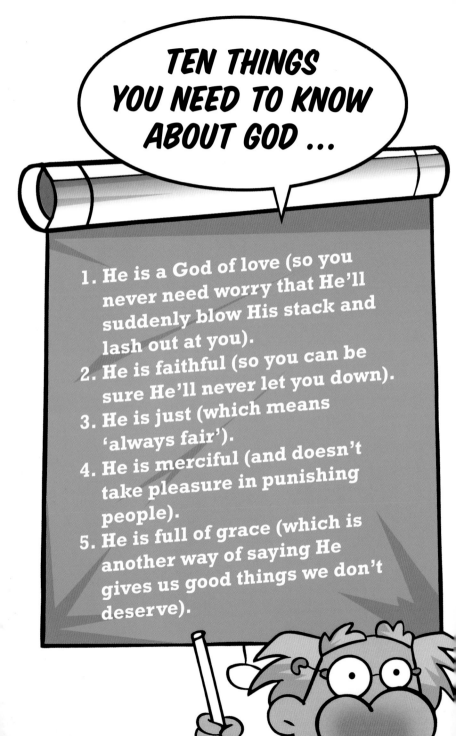

6. He is holy (that means He's perfect and pure).
7. He is righteous (which means He does what is right and never does wrong).
8. He is forgiving (so when we say sorry to God, He never holds a grudge).
9. He is generous (and wants to provide all that we need).
10. He is unchangeable (that means we can always rely on Him).

Now, as I have very helpfully informed you, God can be everywhere at one and the same time.
Amazing I know, but true.

This means that although God lives in heaven, He can also show up down here on the earth as well without even breaking a sweat.
A few thousand years ago, God did exactly that, and in a very special way.
What am I talking about?
I will tell you.

All the while they were in the desert, the Hebrews lived in tents.

GUESS WHO ELSE LIVED IN A TENT?

God did.
He got the
Hebrews to build
Him a top of the
range tent (called
the tabernacle) so
that He could live
slap-bang in the middle of their camp
and be a part of their lives.

Whenever the Hebrews moved on, they took God's tent with them and set it up at their next stop.

When the Hebrews eventually put down roots in Canaan, they built comfy stone houses for themselves and replaced the tabernacle with a super-duper stone building for God to live in.

This was called the Temple, and once a year one of the Hebrews (the high priest) met with God inside the Temple to offer sacrifices to Him.

These days God doesn't live in a tent *or* a temple. Amazing as it might seem, He now lives in people who love Him.

How does He do that?
It's in the Person of the Holy Spirit. Remember me telling you about Him earlier? Glad you were listening.

The God who now makes His home in people like you and me is the very same God that we've looked at in this book because (as the Bible tells us) He's a God who never changes.
That's reassuring, isn't it?
If you fancy yourself as a bit of an amateur detective, why not do some investigating of your own (in the Bible) to find out even more fascinating things about God.

I trust that reading this book has been both informative and educational, and that my cabbage sized brain has not made it too difficult for you to understand.
Until next time, young reader, goodbye!

National Distributors

UK: (and countries not listed below)
CWR, Waverley Abbey House, Waverley Lane, Farnham, Surrey GU9 8EP.
Tel: (01252) 784700 Outside UK (44) 1252 784700 Email: mail@cwr.org.uk

AUSTRALIA: KI Entertainment, Unit 21 317-321 Woodpark Road, Smithfield, New South Wales 2164.
Tel: 1 800 850 777 Fax: 02 9604 3699 Email: sales@kientertainment.com.au

CANADA: David C Cook Distribution Canada, PO Box 98, 55 Woodslee Avenue, Paris,
Ontario N3L 3E5. Tel: 1800 263 2664 Email: swansons@cook.ca

GHANA: Challenge Enterprises of Ghana, PO Box 5723, Accra. Tel: (021) 222437/223249
Fax: (021) 226227 Email: ceg@africaonline.com.gh

HONG KONG: Cross Communications Ltd, 1/F, 562A Nathan Road, Kowloon.
Tel: 2780 1188 Fax: 2770 6229 Email: cross@crosshk.com

INDIA: Crystal Communications, 10-3-18/4/1, East Marredpalli, Secunderabad – 500026, Andhra Pradesh.
Tel/Fax: (040) 27737145 Email: crystal_edwj@rediffmail.com

KENYA: Keswick Books and Gifts Ltd, PO Box 10242-00400, Nairobi.
Tel: (254) 20 312639/3870125 Email: keswick@swiftkenya.com

MALAYSIA: Canaanland, No. 25 Jalan PJU 1A/41B, NZX Commercial Centre, Ara Jaya, 47301 Petaling Jaya,
Selangor. Tel: (03) 7885 0540/1/2 Fax: (03) 7885 0545 Email: info@canaanland.com.my

Salvation Book Centre (M) Sdn Bhd, 23 Jalan SS 2/64, 47300 Petaling Jaya, Selangor.
Tel: (03) 78766411/78766797 Fax: (03) 78757066/78756360
Email: info@salvationbookcentre.com

NEW ZEALAND: KI Entertainment, Unit 21 317-321 Woodpark Road, Smithfield,
New South Wales 2164, Australia. Tel: 0 800 850 777 Fax: +612 9604 3699
Email: sales@kientertainment.com.au

NIGERIA: FBFM, Helen Baugh House, 96 St Finbarr's College Road, Akoka, Lagos.
Tel: (01) 7747429/4700218/825775/827264 Email: fbfm@hyperia.com

PHILIPPINES: OMF Literature Inc, 776 Boni Avenue, Mandaluyong City.
Tel: (02) 531 2183 Fax: (02) 531 1960 Email: gloadlaon@omflit.com

SINGAPORE: Alby Commercial Enterprises Pte Ltd, 95 Kallang Avenue #04-00, AIS Industrial Building, 339420.
Tel: (65) 629 27238 Fax: (65) 629 27235 Email: marketing@alby.com.sg

SOUTH AFRICA: Struik Christian Books, 80 MacKenzie Street, PO Box 1144, Cape Town 8000.
Tel: (021) 462 4360 Fax: (021) 461 3612 Email: info@struikchristianmedia.co.za

SRI LANKA: Christombu Publications (Pvt) Ltd, Bartleet House, 65 Braybrooke Place, Colombo 2.
Tel: (9411) 2421073/2447665 Email: dhanad@bartleet.com

USA: David C Cook Distribution Canada, PO Box 98, 55 Woodslee Avenue, Paris, Ontario N3L 3E5, Canada.
Tel: 1800 263 2664 Email: swansons@cook.ca

CWR is a Registered Charity – Number 294387
CWR is a Limited Company registered in England – Registration Number 1990308

More from Andy Robb!

The Bible is not an easy book to understand if you don't know where to start.

That's why Andy Robb has picked out some of the most exciting stories for you and told them in his own wacky way – which certainly won't leave you bored!

Each story has a cliffhanger ending – and a short Bible passage to look up so you can find out what happened next.

112-page paperbacks, 197x129mm

50 Goriest Bible Stories
Cain and Abel, Abraham and Isaac, Moses and his rebellious relations, David and Goliath, Judas and more.
ISBN: 978-1-85345-530-8

50 Weirdest Bible Stories
The Red Sea crossing, Jesus heals a paralysed man, manna in the desert, the dreams of Joseph, Peter walking on water and more.
ISBN: 978-1-85345-489-9

50 Wildest Bible Stories
Ruth and Boaz, Samson killing a lion with his bare hands, the Queen of Sheba's visit to Solomon, Jesus' temptation by Satan, Paul's angelic visit onboard a ship and more.
ISBN: 978-1-85345-529-2

50 Craziest Bible Stories
Jonah and the big fish, Elijah and the prophets of Baal, Balaam and the donkey, the feeding of the 5,000, Jesus' resurrection, the beggar at the Beautiful Gate and more.
ISBN: 978-1-85345-490-5

MORE FROM THE PROFESSOR!

Who's the bravest? Who's the funniest? Who's the jammiest? Who's the strongest?

Where to start? Join Professor Bumblebrain, self-confessed Bible boffin, for a whistle-stop tour of the heroes and heroines of Bible times.

At his exciting award ceremony, The Bumblebrains, we're introduced to a star-studded line-up: Deborah, Elijah, Jehu, David, Mary, John the Baptist and many others, who all, in one way or another, were heroes for God.

Professor Bumblebrain's Bonkers Book on Bible Heroes
by Andy Robb
100-page paperback,
197x129mm
ISBN: 978-1-85345-578-0